DK SUPER Planet

Who's Eating Who?

Feed your brain by learning all about our planet's fascinating food chains, from plants to predators

Produced for DK by
Editorial Just Content Limited
Design Studio Noel

Author Elizabeth Gilbert Bedia

Senior Editor Ankita Awasthi Tröger
Senior Art Editor Gilda Pacitti
Managing Editor Carine Tracanelli
Managing Art Editor Sarah Corcoran
Production Editor Jaypal Chauhan
DTP Designer Rohit Singh
Production Controller Rebecca Parton
Publisher Sarah Forbes
Managing Director, Learning Hilary Fine

First American Edition, 2025
Published in the United States by DK Publishing,
a division of Penguin Random House LLC
1745 Broadway, 20th Floor, New York, NY 10019

Copyright © 2025 Dorling Kindersley Limited
25 26 27 28 29 10 9 8 7 6 5 4 3 2 1
001–345407–Apr/2025

All rights reserved.
Without limiting the rights under the copyright reserved
above, no part of this publication may be reproduced, stored
in or introduced into a retrieval system, or transmitted, in any
form, or by any means (electronic, mechanical, photocopying,
recording, or otherwise), without the prior written permission
of the copyright owner.
Published in Great Britain by Dorling Kindersley Limited

A catalog record for this book
is available from the Library of Congress.
HC ISBN: 978-0-5939-6254-1
PB ISBN: 978-0-5939-6253-4

DK books are available at special discounts when purchased
in bulk for sales promotions, premiums, fund-raising,
or educational use.
For details, contact: DK Publishing Special Markets,
1745 Broadway, 20th Floor, New York, NY 10019
SpecialSales@dk.com

Printed and bound in China

www.dk.com

Contents

Food for Life	4
What is a Food Chain?	6
Who "Eats" the Sun's Energy?	8
Starting the Chain: Plentiful Plants	10
Who Eats Plants?	12
Bamboo for Breakfast: Panda	14
Who Eats Herbivores?	16
Deadly Ambush: Praying Mantis	18
Who Eats Carnivores?	20
What a Shock: Electric Eel	22
Who Eats Everything Else?	24
Clever Killer: Orca	26
Discovering Decomposers	28
Energy Transfers	30
Food Webs	32
Unbalanced Ecosystems	34
Everyday Science: Plant Protein	36
Everyday Science: Indoor Microfarms	38
Let's Experiment! Wiggly Wormery	40
Vocabulary Builder: Breaking News	42
Glossary	44
Index	46

Words in **bold** are explained in the glossary on page 44.

Food for Life

Every living thing on Earth needs food. Food provides **energy** that living things need to grow and survive. Plants get their food from the Sun, air, water, and soil. Animals get their food from plants and other animals.

Hummingbirds have an extremely high **metabolism**. They need around 5,000 calories per day. That is more than two times the daily calories of a human.

Dung beetles eat animal **dung**. They are the strongest animals in the world. Male dung beetles can pull over 1,000 times their own body weight.

Tropical jungles contain a huge amount of different plants and animals. The jungle provides them with all they need to survive.

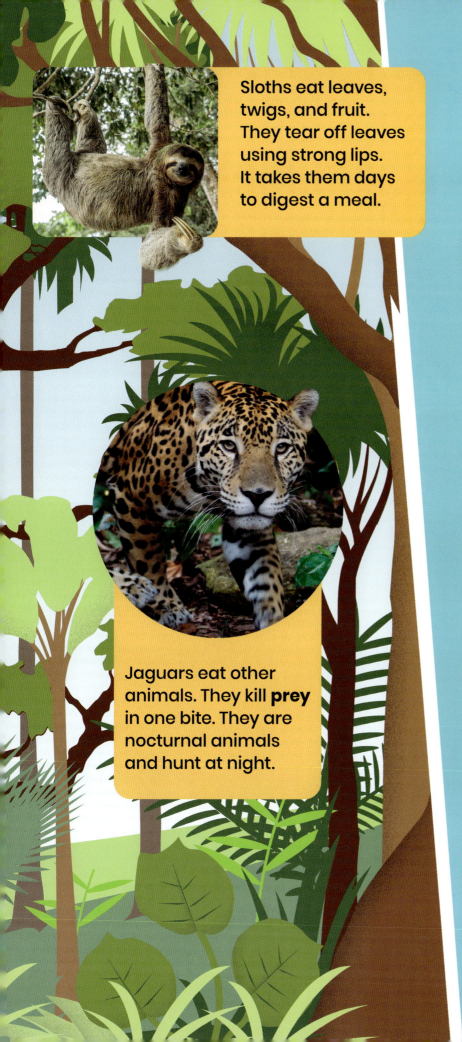

Sloths eat leaves, twigs, and fruit. They tear off leaves using strong lips. It takes them days to digest a meal.

Jaguars eat other animals. They kill **prey** in one bite. They are nocturnal animals and hunt at night.

Ocean menus

Blue whales are the largest animals on Earth. They eat tiny krill. Blue whales can eat

35,000 lb (16,000 kg)

of krill in one day.

That is like you eating

35,000 loaves

of bread in one day!

What is a Food Chain?

All living things depend on other plants and animals to survive. Plants and animals are connected to each other in **food chains**. A food chain is a diagram. It uses arrows to show how energy from food moves from one living thing to another in an **ecosystem**.

Apex predators are consumers at the top of a food chain. They get their energy by eating other animals. Eagles are apex predators.

Fascinating fact

Human activity can have a huge effect on food chains. This includes **pollution**, hunting, and destroying **habitats**.

Frogs are consumers. They get their energy by eating other animals.

Plants are **producers**. They make their own food using energy from the Sun.

Grasshoppers are **consumers**. They need to find food instead of making it. Grasshoppers get energy by eating plants.

Snakes are also consumers. They get their energy by eating other animals.

Predators and prey

Food chains keep ecosystems healthy. If there are too many consumers, it can throw the system out of balance. Food chains are made up of many **predators** and **prey** animals.

Predators hunt and eat other smaller animals.

Prey animals are hunted and eaten by predators.

7

Who "Eats" the Sun's Energy?

All plants need energy from the Sun to survive.

The source of all energy on Earth is the Sun. Without it, there would be no plants. And there would be no food chains! Plants are the very first part of a food chain. Unlike animals, they mostly don't eat other living things. Instead, plants use energy from the Sun to make their own food. This process is known as photosynthesis. Living things that make their own food are known as producers.

The leaves take in energy from the Sun.

The roots take in water from the soil.

The stem then carries water from the roots to the leaves.

Plants need water and **nutrients** from the soil to grow well.

8

How plants spread

Plants have many clever ways to spread their seeds and establish themselves.

Some plants have small, light seeds that can be **dispersed** by the wind. Dandelion seeds have feathery bristles that help them float away. Other plants have seeds that spin as they fly, or seeds with wings that help them flutter to the ground.

Another way for some plants to spread is by water. Coconuts are heavy but float well and are carried long distances by the sea.

Some plants are spread by animals. When birds eat berries, the seeds inside are spread to new places by the bird's poop.

Starting the Chain: Plentiful Plants

Plants come in all shapes and sizes. They can be found all around the world in almost every environment, even in very hot or cold places. They take their energy from the Sun and are producers—the start of most food chains. Let's explore some different types of producers.

Green algae grow in both fresh and salt water. Even under the water, algae such as mermaid's wineglass *(above)* take in energy from the Sun. Algae provide food for many creatures, including fish, insects, and water birds.

Mosses are small plants that grow in damp, shady areas. They have been growing on Earth for about 450 million years. Mosses are found all over the world.

Some plants produce seeds in cones. This group of plants includes conifers such as cedars (*right*). Conifers grow needles rather than large leaves. They can be found all over the world. Some conifers produce berries and nuts, which are important food sources for animals.

Find out!

Can you find one example of each of these types of plants in your local area?

Flowering plants grow on land and in water. They are important food sources for animals, fish, and insects. The leaves and flowers of water lilies (*below*) float on the water.

Ferns can be found in a wide range of places, including tropical rainforests, bogs, and on trees. They can be tiny plants or as big as a tree.

Who Eats Plants?

Food chains start with plants. But unlike plants, animals cannot make their own food. They are consumers—they need to find food to eat instead of making it. **Herbivores** are a type of consumer that only eat plants. Let's discover different types of herbivores.

There are over 16 million cows in the Great Plains. Cows mostly eat grass.

Abalone live in the seas off California and eat kelp and algae. Their numbers dropped due to overfishing, disease, and climate change. Fishing was stopped to help them recover.

Monarch caterpillars only eat milkweed leaves. They are only found where milkweed grows, including North and South America and Australia.

Arctic

In the winter, the arctic hare digs through snow to find plants.

Australia

Koalas in Australia mostly eat the leaves of the eucalyptus tree.

Hungry plants!

All plants are producers. But a few plants get food from animals too.

Venus fly traps are plants that eat insects. They are found on the east coast of the US.

Pitcher plants are found in tropical and wetland areas where the soil is too poor for most plants. Some even eat animals as big as rats!

Bamboo for Breakfast: Panda

Giant pandas are herbivores. They spend up to 16 hours a day eating bamboo. Bamboo does not contain much energy so pandas have to eat a lot of it. Today, there are only around 1,800 giant pandas left in the wild.

Scientists believe that long ago, giant pandas were **carnivores**. Today, they eat mainly bamboo leaves, stems, and shoots.

Fascinating fact

A huge 99 percent of a giant panda's diet is bamboo and other plants.

In the wild, giant pandas live in massive bamboo forests in China.

Giant pandas are essential to their food chain. By spreading the seeds of bamboo and other plants in their dung, they help bamboo grow.

Saving pandas

For several years, giant pandas were **endangered**. But thanks to **conservation**, this is no longer the case.

Many giant pandas live on special nature reserves.

Conservationists have helped pandas reproduce in captivity so they can be released into the wild.

Who Eats Herbivores?

In a food chain, consumers are animals that eat other animals. They can be carnivores, **omnivores**, or **insectivores**. Carnivores eat mostly meat. Omnivores eat meat and plants. And insectivores eat mostly insects. Consumers can be found in food chains all around the world, from the Arctic to tropical coral reefs.

Phytoplankton are at the bottom of the food chain. They are producers and get their energy from the Sun.

Zooplankton are consumers. They are herbivores and get their energy by eating phytoplankton.

Apex predators such as polar bears are also consumers. They are at the top of the food chain.

Cod and seals are consumers. They are carnivores and get their energy by eating other animals.

Find out!

From how far away can a polar bear smell a seal above the ice?

Up to 20 miles (32 km) away.

Underwater food chains

Some food chains are found entirely in the oceans. Sea anemones are colorful animals that live in oceans and seas around the world.

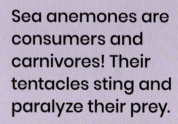

Sea anemones are consumers and carnivores! Their tentacles sting and paralyze their prey.

Clownfish shelter in anemones. Waste from the clownfish provides anemones with food.

Deadly Ambush: Praying Mantis

Praying mantises are skilled hunters. These insects are carnivores that live in warm climates around the world. Although only a couple of inches long, they can hunt prey three times their size. They eat insects, spiders, birds, and small reptiles. Females even eat their male mates.

Praying mantises have strong, flexible forearms with sharp edges for attacking their prey. They eat their prey while it is still alive.

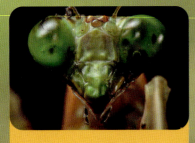

Praying mantises have enormous **compound eyes** that allow them to see in 3D (three dimensions).

Fascinating fact

Táng Láng Quán (Northern Praying Mantis Kung Fu) is a martial art based on the movements of the praying mantis.

Praying mantises can **camouflage** themselves to surprise their prey.

When praying mantises ambush their prey, it is so fast that you can't see it.

The ghost mantis lives in Africa. It looks like a dried-up leaf.

Who Eats Carnivores?

Consumers who eat other animals are called carnivores. Some types of carnivores eat herbivores, some eat other carnivores, and some eat both. Carnivores are predators. This means they hunt other animals, known as prey. Every food chain is made up of predators and prey.

Grasses are the producers at the start of this food chain.

Crickets are omnivores, eating plants and other insects.

Frogs are mostly carnivorous, eating insects such as crickets.

Jaguars eat other carnivores. They have teeth and jaws strong enough to bite through the thick skin of crocodiles and caimans.

Crocodiles hide their bodies underwater and watch out for prey. Only their eyes, nostrils, and ears are exposed until they leap out to attack their prey.

Antarctic carnivores

Many of the carnivores that live in the Antarctic get their energy from animals that live in the sea.

Emperor penguins hunt for silverfish in Antarctica. They use their sight and dive deep.

Southern elephant seals are named for their trunk-like nose. They eat fish, squid, and krill.

Both seals and penguins eat squid. Squid are carnivores that eat fish and shrimp-like animals. Some squid even eat other squid!

Fascinating fact

Crocodiles haven't changed much from their early relatives. Prehistoric alligators lived around 95 million years ago. They were water-dwelling carnivores with lots of teeth.

21

What a Shock: Electric Eel

Electric eels are amazing predators. But despite their name they are actually fish, and are related to catfish and carp. Unlike other fish, they need to surface regularly to breathe air. This helps them to survive in slow, murky waters.

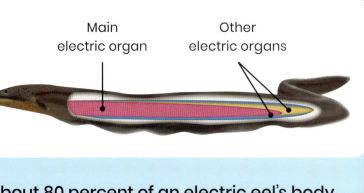

About 80 percent of an electric eel's body is made up of organs that generate electricity. These are shown in pink, blue, and yellow in the picture (*above*).

Fascinating fact

Electric eels can send 600 volts of electricity into their prey or into a predator. That is more than five times the amount in a standard wall outlet.

Electric eels are native to South America. They can grow up to 8 ft (2.4 m) long!

Balancing ecosystems

Electric eels are an important part of their food chains.

Electric eels are carnivores. Their diet includes fish, insects, and even some mammals.

Big predators help balance ecosystems. Electric eel shocks keep away other predators like caimans. This stops there being too many animals at the top of the food chain.

Who Eats Everything Else?

Apex predators are very important to food chains. They control the numbers of other animals in the food chain and this helps to balance the ecosystem.

Apex predators are animals at the top of their food chain. This means they have no natural predators, although they can be threatened by humans. Competition for food at the top of the food chain is fierce. Apex predators have to defend their homes so they and their young can survive.

Apex predators like grizzly bears eat other consumers in the food chain. But no other animal eats apex predators.

Fascinating fact

At the end of summer grizzly bears will eat for 20 hours a day to store energy for winter.

Tasmanian devils can eat much bigger animals such as sheep and even kangaroos.

The giant Pacific octopus surprises its prey and injects venom to paralyze it.

American alligators hide in water before attacking their target. Adults can catch and eat prey of almost any size.

Lions like to hunt during storms. The noise and wind makes it harder for their prey to see and hear the lions.

Wolves hunt their prey over long distances. They wait for the perfect opportunity to attack.

Some people see humans as apex predators, too. Humans eat plants and animals—we are omnivores.

Clever Killer: Orca

Orcas (also known as killer whales) are some of the most intelligent and social animals on Earth. They are not actually whales, but a type of dolphin. These fearsome apex predators live and hunt together in groups called pods. They communicate with each other using clicks, calls, and whistles.

Orcas are carnivores that mostly eat mammals, including sea lions, seals, and even whales. They can jump out of the water to knock seals into the sea.

Fascinating fact

Each half of an orca's brain takes turns sleeping. This way, they know when to come up to the surface to breathe. They even keep the eye on the awake side open.

Discovering Decomposers

Living things that break down and eat the leftovers in a food chain are known as **decomposers**. These leftovers include dung, dead plants, and dead animals. By breaking down this dead **matter**, decomposers put nutrients back into the soil. This keeps the food chain balanced and the ecosystem healthy.

While earthworms do eat dead animals, they mostly eat dead leaves and plants. Their dung adds nutrients back into the soil.

Millipedes have a hard shell. Most have fewer than 100 legs, but some have almost 1,000. They eat dead and decaying plants.

The rhinoceros beetle is one of the strongest beetles in the world. It can lift up to 850 times its own body weight. The **larvae** live on dead, rotten wood.

Find out!

Can you find out the names of three decomposers living in your area?

Fungi are important decomposers. Some fungi glow a neon-green color at night.

Bacteria are very tiny living things. The soil contains many bacteria. They break down dead animals and plants.

Some earthworms can grow up to

14 in (35.5 cm)

long. That is more than the height of a cereal box!

Most fungi are tiny. There are over

50,000

kinds of fungi around the world.

Energy Transfers

Food is energy. Food chains show how energy flows from producers to consumers. Consumers use the energy to hunt for prey, escape from predators, and produce young. At each level of a food chain, most of the energy available at that level is used up—only a small amount flows up to the next level.

The Sun is the source of all energy in food chains on our planet.

Find out!

Can you draw a simple food chain of one plant and some animals that live in your area?

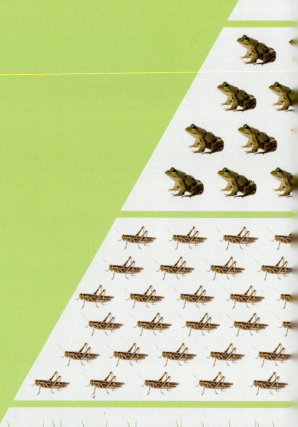

Finally, a small amount of this energy flows to apex predators. This food chain supports one eagle.

A small amount of this energy flows further up to the next level of consumers. This food chain supports 10 snakes.

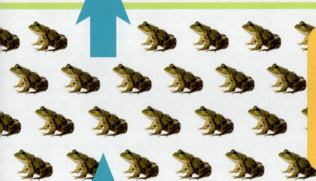

A small amount of this energy then flows up to the next level of consumers. This food chain supports 100 frogs.

A small amount of this energy flows up to consumers, who eat producers. This food chain supports 1,000 grasshoppers.

Energy from the Sun flows to producers. This food chain starts with 10,000 blades of grass.

Energy from the Sun

Food Webs

All the food chains in an ecosystem make up a **food web**. Animals eat many different things, whether they are herbivores, omnivores, or carnivores. What an animal eats depends on the food that is available in its ecosystem. Follow the arrows to find the producers and consumers in this food web.

Find out!

Can you draw a food web of an ecosystem? You could choose the ocean, desert, or even your own backyard or local park.

Bushes and trees

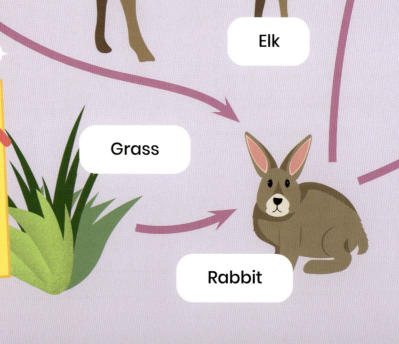
Bear

Elk

Grass

Rabbit

Wolf

Coyote

Salmon

Otter

Wolves are apex predators. They are carnivores. They hunt elk, otters, and hares.

Elk are herbivores. They eat grass and berries.

Brown bears are also apex predators. They are omnivores. They hunt salmon and elk, and also eat berries.

Unbalanced Ecosystems

Around the world, ecosystems that are strong can survive many changes. But some changes are so big that they make the ecosystem unbalanced. Examples of these big changes include **climate change**, pollution, and habitat destruction.

Ocean pollution is leading to sea turtles eating and getting tangled up in plastics. This causes some turtles to get hurt and even die.

Insects such as monarch butterflies are dying off. This is caused by the destruction of their habitats, use of **pesticides**, and climate change.

Fascinating fact

Ecosystems are not just found in the wild. Big cities are also ecosystems. Raccoons, possums, pigeons, and foxes may live there.

Around the world, ocean temperatures are increasing due to climate change. This is killing krill. Emperor penguins need the krill to survive.

Balancing ecosystems

You can make a difference to the ecosystems where you live.

Cut down on plastic pollution by avoiding plastic packaging.

Recycle paper, aluminum, glass, and plastic so they do not get thrown away into landfill.

Planting wildflowers at your home or school will help honeybees and other insects.

Plant a fruit and vegetable garden. It can provide food for people, animals, and decomposers.

Everyday Science

Plant Protein

Today, more and more people are eating plant-based diets. This means that instead of eating meat, they eat foods made from plants. Many of these foods have similar nutrients to meat, including protein, vitamins, minerals, fat, and water. These foods can sometimes even look and taste like meat. Eating meat alternatives can help the environment by saving water, reducing pollution, and protecting nature.

Wheat, like all grains, is a grass. It is one of the oldest crops in the world and is a good source of nutrients.

Growing plants uses less land and water than raising livestock. It releases fewer **greenhouse gases** into the air.

Eating vegetables, fruits, and whole grains improves people's health.

Cows release methane into the air. Methane is a greenhouse gas that speeds up climate change.

Animals raised for meat have to eat a lot of plants to survive. This means that farmers need to turn wild areas, like forests and other natural habitats, into farmland. This also speeds up climate change.

Protein power

Plants can give you almost all the nutrients your body needs to survive.

Meat contains protein, an important nutrient needed by our bodies. Beans, soybeans, and nuts have protein too.

Tofu is a plant protein that is made from soybeans. It was first made in China in the 2nd century CE.

Everyday **Science**

Indoor Microfarms

Farming has been around for thousands of years. But today, innovative growing methods have made it easier to buy fresh, healthy food. Indoor microfarms grow fresh vegetables, fruits, herbs, and flowers closer to home. They give us fresh produce all year round, even in cold winter months.

Indoor farms come in all sizes, from large commercial farms to tiny indoor gardens in people's homes.

Special lighting is used by indoor farms. It is very similar to sunlight and allows the plants to grow.

Indoor farms control their light, water, humidity, and temperature. Poor weather does not damage indoor plants and fewer pesticides are needed.

Then...

Traditional farming uses methods like hand-sowing and hand-tilling. It does not rely on technology.

Now...

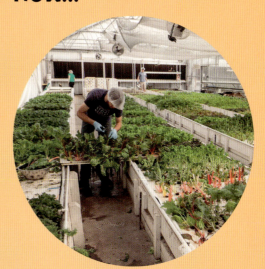

Modern farming uses technology to help crops grow bigger and faster in different conditions.

Let's Experiment!

Wiggly Wormery

Earthworms are decomposers. They eat dead leaves, plants, and animal matter. You can see this in action by making your own wormery. The type of worm you will need is *Eisenia fetida*, often called brandling, red, tiger, or manure worm.

You will need:
- A clear container and some worms
- Sand and soil
- Dead leaves and vegetable peelings
- A watering can and a trowel
- Sticky tape and some black cardboard

Make sure you wash your hands after handling the worms and soil.

1 Fill a clear, empty container with alternating layers of soil and thinner layers of sand.

2 Cover with peelings and dead leaves.

3 Gently place your worms on the top. Let the worms tunnel into the soil.

4 Cover the container with black cardboard. Secure the cardboard with tape. Water the pot 1–2 times a week. After two weeks, see what's happened!

HEALTHY SOIL

Earthworms help keep soil healthy. They break down dead matter into smaller pieces. Bacteria and fungi break these pieces down even more.

Vocabulary Builder
Breaking News

Axolotls are endangered amphibians that are only found in Mexico City. Read the interview to hear about why axolotls are at risk, and why the species is important to its ecosystem.

 This is Monarch Butterfly reporting live from Mexico. I'm here with Axolotl. She's worried about her ecosystem.

We axolotls used to live in all the freshwater canals here. But now, we're really endangered. There are only about 1,000 of us left in the wild.

 Axolotls are salamanders native to Mexico. They eat insects, mollusks, worms, and fish. Axolotls hide from their predators among plants in lakes and canals. Back to you, Axolotl.

We use energy to reproduce, hunt, and hide from predators. We can even grow back body parts!

 Thank you for your time today, Axolotl. Good luck!

Choose an animal you know about, or research one. Then use the interview on page 42 and the prompts and word bank below to write your own interview.

- What are some of the things it does every day?
- What does it need in order to thrive and what dangers does it face?
- Why is it important to its ecosystem?

What animals do	communicate	hide	reproduce
	eat	hunt	sleep
	grow	live	survive

What animals need	ecosystem	habitat	prey
	energy	insects	shelter
	food	plants	water

Threats animals face	climate change	habitat loss	hunting
	disease	humans	pollution
	extinction	hunger	predators

Glossary

Apex predator A consumer at the top of its food chain that has no natural predators.

Camouflage An animal's ability to blend in with its surroundings, used either to hide from predators or to hunt prey.

Carnivore An animal that only eats other animals.

Climate change Long-term changes in Earth's weather patterns and temperatures that are happening around the world.

Compound eye A type of eye made up of hundreds or thousands of tiny light-sensitive parts, with each part creating part of an image.

Conservation Working to protect the environment along with the animals and plants that live in it.

Conservationist Someone who works in conservation.

Consumer A living thing that eats producers or other consumers.

Decomposer A living thing that can break down dead plants or animals and recycles (returns) these nutrients back into the soil.

Dispersed When something is moved away to a new place.

Dung Animal poop.

Ecosystem A community of plants, animals, and other living things that interact with non-living things in their environment.

Endangered An animal that is at risk of going extinct.

Energy The ability to make things happen and cause changes.

Food chain A chain that shows the relationship between all the plants and animals in an ecosystem and illustrates how energy is transferred between them.

Food web A web made up of many different food chains that shows the relationships between plants and animals in an ecosystem.

Fungi A special group of living things that are neither plants, animals, nor bacteria. Mushrooms are fungi. They get food from decomposing organic matter. Just one is called a fungus.

Greenhouse gas A gas in Earth's atmosphere that traps heat and makes Earth hotter.

Habitat The natural home of a plant, animal, or any living thing.

Herbivore An animal that eats only plants.

Insectivore An animal that mostly or only eats insects.

Larvae The young of insects. A caterpillar is a larva.

Matter Any substance that takes up space.

Metabolism The process in which living things change food into energy.

Nutrient A substance that helps plants and animals survive and grow.

Omnivore An animal that eats both plants and animals.

Pesticide A chemical that people use to kill weeds and pests (such as some insects) that may harm farm crops.

Pollution Releasing a harmful substance into the environment. Pollution can happen to the air, water, or on land.

Predator An animal that hunts and eats other animals.

Prey An animal that is hunted and eaten by other animals.

Producer A living thing that uses energy from the Sun to make its own food. A plant is a producer.

Recycle To collect materials that otherwise would be thrown away as trash in order to turn them into new products. Glass, metal, and paper are easy to recycle.

School A group of fish that swim together.

Index

A
acorns 9
algae 10
alligators 20, 25
Antarctica 21
apex predators 6, 17, 24–27
Arctic 13
arctic hares 13
Australia 13
axolotls 44–45

B
bacteria 29, 41
bamboo 14–15
beans 37
bears 17, 24, 33
black bears 33
blue whales 5

C
cacti 8
caimans 23
carnivores 16, 20–21
cherry trees 8
climate change 34, 37
clownfish 17
coconuts 9
cod 17
conifers 11
conservation, giant pandas 15
consumers 6, 7, 16, 17, 20
cows 12, 37
coyotes 33
crickets 20
crocodiles 20–21

D
dandelions 9
decomposers 28–29
dung beetles 4

E
eagles 6, 31
earthworms 28, 29
   wormery 40–41
ecosystems, unbalanced 34–35
electric eels 22–23
elk 32
emperor penguins 21, 35
energy transfers 30–31

F
farms 38–39
ferns 11
flowering plants 11
food 4–5
   energy transfers 30–31
food chains 6–7
   carnivores 20–21
   herbivores 16–17
   start of 8–9
food webs 32–33
frogs 7, 20, 31
fungi 29, 41

G
gardens 13
ghost mantises 19
giant Pacific octopuses 25
giant pandas 14–15
grass 20, 31, 32, 36
grasshoppers 6, 31
great white sharks 27
greenhouse gas 36, 37
grizzly bears 24

H
herbivores 16–17
herring 27
honeybees 13
humans 6, 25
hummingbirds 4

I, J
insectivores 16
jaguars 5, 21
jungles 4

K
kelp 10, 12
killer whales *see* orcas
koalas 13
krill 5, 35

L, M
lions 25
meat 37
microfarms 38–9
milkweed 12
millipedes 28
monarch caterpillars and butterflies 12, 34, 44
mosses 10

N
North America 12
nuts 37

O
oceans 34, 35
omnivores 16

orcas (killer whales) 26–27
otters 33

P
photosynthesis 8
phytoplankton 16
pitcher plants 13
plants 6, 10–11, 32
　food 12–13, 36–37
　in the food chain 8–9
polar bears 17, 24
pollution 34, 36
praying mantises 18–19
predators 7, 20, 31
prey 7, 20
producers 6
protein, plant 36–37

R
rabbits 32
rhinoceros beetle 28

S
salmon 33
sea anemones 17
seals 17, 21, 26
sea urchins 12

seed dispersal 9
seeds, producers 11
sloths 5
snakes 7, 31
Southern elephant seals 21
soybeans 37
squid 21
squirrels 9
Sun 8–9, 10, 30, 31

T
Tasmanian devils 25
tofu 37
turtles 34

U
underwater food chains 17

V
Venus fly traps 13

W, Z
wheat 36
wolves 25, 33
wormery experiment 40–41
zooplankton 16

Acknowledgments

The publisher would like to thank the following for their kind permission to reproduce their photographs:

(Key: a-above; b-below/bottom; c-center; f-far; l-left; r-right; t-top)

123RF.com: Melinda Fawver / epantha 7bl, 30-31 (Snake), Carolyn Franks 37bc, hanohiki 4bc; **Adobe Stock:** Aliaksei 14tr, Simon Kovacic 18-19, James Stone 25tl, Todd Winner 17br; **Alamy Stock Photo:** All Canada Photos / Kitchin and Hurst 34b, All Canada Photos / Rolf Hicker 27crb, anjahennern 13br, Putu Artana 18clb, Arterra Picture Library / Clement Philippe 28tr, Jean-Paul Ferrero / AUSCAPE 5crb, blickwinkel / F. Teigler 43, blickwinkel / M. Woike 25cl, Robert D Brozek 12tr, Keren Su / China Span 5cl, Don Johnston_MA 7bc, Sue Flood 35cl, Imagebroker / Arco / G. Lacz 13bl, Imagebroker / Arco / O. Diez 35br, Imaginechina 15br, Ernie Janes 13tr, Jeffrey Isaac Greenberg 19+ 39tr, Philip Lehman 35bc, Don Hooper / LOOP IMAGES 7br, Natural Visions / Heather Angel 15bl, Nature Picture Library / Tony Wu 27tr, Niebrugge Images 25tr, Adisha Pramod 22bl, Jon Reaves 33cr, Jeff Rotman 17cra, Kay Roxby 38bc, Photostock-Israel / Science Photo Library 24bl, Steve Gschmeissner / Science Photo Library 29bl, Martin Shields 12br, Tom Stack 12bl, Rosanne Tackaberry 15tr, VPC Animals Photo 22-23, WaterFrame_dpr 27br, 35tr, WaterFrame_fba 5tr, 23crb, Jim West 39br, David Wogan 33tr; **Depositphotos Inc:** herraez 21tc; **Dorling Kindersley:** Thomas Marent 19tr; **Dreamstime.com:** Beata Becla / Acik 36br, Steve Allen 7tr, Andreanita 24br, Tony Campbell 13tl, Razvan Cornel Constantin 19cr, Rudmer Zwerver / Creativenature1 28bc, Davemhuntphotography 19br, Diadis 11cl, Ika Djodjiro 36tr, David Franklin 15tl, Gbruev 30tr, Jakub Gojda 34crb, Ioana Grecu 10br, Antonio Guillem 33br, Nina Hilitukha 39clb, Hospitalera 11tr, Isselee 6br, 30-31 (Frog), Jerryway 42l, Kelpfish 17ca, Kjetil Kolbjornsrud 25bl, Ferenc Kósa 11br, Ashish Kumar 10tr, Landfillgirl 9br, Mattiaath 18tr, Pranodh Mongkolthavorn 37l, Duncan Noakes 4cl, Paddyman2013 29cla, Perambulator 28cl, Photographyfirm 41br, Piolka 6bl, Alexander Podshivalov / Withgod 6tr, 31tl, Pressmaster 38-39, Reimarg 23tr, Sahua 9tr, Skynetphoto 6bc, 30-31 (Grasshopper), Simone Gatterwe / Smgirly 26-27ca, Alex Bramwell / Spanishalex 9bc, Aleksandra Suzi 35cr, Johannes Gerhardus Swanepoel 25cr, Manfred Thuerig 21tr, Valya82 8bc, Goinyk Volodymyr 14bl, Bogdan Wakowicz 29crb, John Williams 29tr, Andrii Yalanskyi 36, Yulianny 37tr; **Getty Images / iStock:** DGLimages 25br, GlobalP 42r, MattCuda 4cr, OperationShooting 23bl, Enrico Pescantini 5tl; **Science Photo Library:** British Antarctic Survey 21br

Cover images: *Back:* **Alamy Stock Photo:** Martin Shields bl; **Dreamstime.com:** Steve Allen cl, Landfillgirl tl